Fire in the Well

Poetry for Women
Awakening the Inner Sage

I0192342

Poems by
Marilyn Loy Every, DMin

For publishing inquiries:
Sapient Publishing
www.Sagessence.com

ISBN: 978-0-9910354-1-0

Library of Congress Data on File with the Publisher

Printed in the USA

10 9 8 7 6 5 4 3 2

Fire in the Well

❀

IS DEDICATED TO

Lavina Christiana Nelsen Foster
(10-22-1904—6-9-2001)

an unpublished poet and songwriter,
artist, philosopher, teacher,
daughter, sister, wife, grandmother,
and my beloved aunt,
who always lovingly believed in me,
and my place in the world.

CONTENTS

Fire in the Well

❀

Contents

✿

ACKNOWLEDGMENTS

Fire in the Well

❀

In discovering and deepening my own unique wisdom gained throughout the decades of my life, poetry has become a rich path of discernment, prayer, creativity and spiritual practice. Clearly, many life experiences have contributed to its texture and evolution. The heartfelt stories of many women have also influenced my writing. I thank each and every woman who shared her story, as I believe all of heaven celebrates whenever another tender heart has been heard through the language of poetry.

I am eternally grateful for my beloved spiritual mentor of many years, Kathleen Fischer, PhD, who relentlessly encouraged me to honor my writing and poetry. Dr. Fischer supported my process to liberate life experiences through narrative poetry as a life-giving spiritual practice. Many thanks to Kim Rosen, MFA, a beautifully seasoned poet and instructor, who taught me to trust my poetry, and to give it honor and expression in the world. My heart is filled with gratitude for Alexandra Kovats, CSJP, who continues to hold a sacred space for my soul to explore creative energies. I am also deeply appreciative for Rev. Lauren Artress, DMin, who masterfully encourages the art of creative practices for my spiritual nourishment.

I treasure the creative spirits of many others who have been and continue to be my mentors, those who breathe with the potency and beauty of poetic expression—from seasoned teachers, so-journeying poet friends, acclaimed poets, and wise women and men who have inspired me on my sacred path. Each has carved a heartfelt and steadfast place in my heart.

INTRODUCTION

Fire in the Well

❁

Women inspirited to live as sages are called to be living examples of personal authenticity, to make vital, life-affirming choices and to live fully emanating wise, compassionate and mentoring spirits. As sage leaders consciously living from the center of their *Sagessence,* they illuminate beauty from feminine fullness and from wisdom gained throughout the sacred journey of their lives. In other words, Sagessence is the illumination of authentic wisdom-in-action shining forth from a woman who lives intentionally as a sage leader.

The ministry of my work is to encourage women to consider and discern their life as a sage. As a woman moves into "fertile maturity" as a sage, she becomes an alchemist. The power of alchemy is the power to be a conscious transformational author of her own life, positively influencing her family, community and the world. As a woman moves from an age when her womb had potential to nourish creations with her life-giving water, into a post-menopausal stage, metaphorically, heat strikes fire deep in the well of her soul for new passions and causes to emerge. A deeper sense of wisdom emerges from this fertile maturity.

My hope is that messages woven throughout *Fire in the Well* will inspire women to recognize and nurture the following themes that may be consciously integrated into their daily lives:

The **Fire of Authenticity** ignites our genuine truth, expands our unique creative potential, nurtures imagination to birth ideas and dreams and inspires liberating images of our lives.

The **Fire of Passion** invites us to live passionately in the moment, to foster love, joy, wonder and gratitude, to deepen pleasures in our living and make vital, life-affirming choices.

The **Fire of Compassion** stirs us to practice loving kindness, to live into the flow of loss, grief and change, to graciously give and receive care and to move through life transitions confidently.

The **Fire of Vision** calls us to create a living legacy that supports greater good, to manifest deeper fulfillment, to impart a wise, mentoring spirit and to honor intergenerational connectedness.

Women can access greater empowerment when they open their hearts to embrace their sacred journey of aging, their ever-transforming nature, unique rhythms and capacity to be inspired. As they foster authenticity, passion, compassion and vision in their lives, they can create expanding opportunities for gratifying change and fulfillment throughout the seasons of life. Thereby, they come to sense that they personally hold the key to the powerful emergence of their own wise sage.

For each person who reads these poems of Sagessence, I encourage taking a few moments to hold each poem contemplatively as a sacred reflection of life. I suggest exploring a vantage point that carries you deeper into your own well of discernment, inspiration, and wisdom. May you begin to recognize your own illumination of wisdom-in-action shining forth into the world. Therefore, in honoring your Sagessence, and celebrating the Sagessence of many other women around the world, I invite you on this journey—**Fire in the Well.**

Fire in the Well
Poetry for Women Awakening the Inner Sage

❀

One Great Mystery

One great mystery
pulses in the well of life
breathing fire in me,
breathing fire in you.

It breathes in the poet,
the poet breathes verse,
verse breathes meaning,
expressing its life.

I sense its words
breathing inside me;
I hear its whispers
of creative desire.

It comes in many ways
trusting I will hear,
I will see, I will feel it;
there is no separation.

It writes, it paints,
sings, draws, composes,
and dances me . . .
dances you.

Continue

Pulsing in the well of life,
one great mystery,
breathing fire in me,
breathing fire in you.

Fire in the Well

✺

Chapter I

Fire of Authenticity

ignites our genuine truth,
expands our unique creative potential,
nurtures imagination to birth ideas and dreams,
and
inspires liberating images of our lives.

Alchemist

I have come to realize
one of the greatest journeys
is one of moving past fear,
accepting with new eyes,
discovering a grander view
that desires expression
in and through my life.

Even when my feet tremble,
heart throbbing in my ears,
I can still hear
that inner voice
urging me
to trust vistas unknown . . .
if I will just surrender.

Whether it be in quietness
or in chaos of uncertainty,
I will again feel
the one thing
that will not
leave me alone . . .
a fire in my belly—

An alchemist leading me on,
melding me into the masterpiece
of an even higher calling . . .
if I will just surrender
to the gods
and drink in trust
like fresh, cool water.

Arrow of Truth

In that moment,
my truth
was like a long,
lean arrow
held back firm
on a red,
willowy bow…
taunt,
as I listened
to my heavy,
halting breath…
hands sweating
as I felt
hard pounding
of my racing heart.

Then, trembling…
release
was direct,
release
was seamless,
slicing
through debris
while the backdraft
lanced my core

with a strike
of pure light.
And, I was swept
by its faithful wind.
And, I was filled
with sweet freedom.

Birth of the Sage

Unlike mother's third babe,
I am now taller with breadth.
I speak my own language,
articulate and confident.
Tracings of age etch my face.
Both palms are now carved
with deep lines of a lifetime.
My heart, under fuller breasts,
nurtures dreams for the world.

Belly now supple, round—
with fullness suggesting yet
another kind of birthing,
I look into the reflection
of my mirrored naked body
uncertain of what is beyond
this incarnate illumination.
It is as if I have conceived
a life I am yet meant to live.

Inside I hear whispers
from a soft, husky voice—
Your time has come.
Let go, surrender to the
powerful pulsing rhythm
urging birth of your sage.

Reconcile the blueprint
of your life, and beget the
path of your woman soul.

Now with womanly fullness,
I sense the inner push of
a profound metamorphosis.
I summon my keen intuition,
open my well-traveled heart,
and claim seasoned wisdom
of a matured woman cloaked
in years of refined texture and
intricate tapestry of a sacred life.

Once again,
I am filled
with another
first precious breath,
and now
I know
my long-awaited sage
has been given
her birth.

Breath of Knowing

There are times a woman
will say, *no,* to those she loves,
carry no judgment of her own,
and in her next breath
affirm, *yes,*
to the bold voice
of the wise sage within.

As for me . . .
I will follow my dreams,
kindly dismiss what no longer
I choose to carry,
let my heart speak its truth,
and give to life the only gift
I have to give—my truest self.

My eyes will be on the owl
as dear ones call out to me,
Please come back . . .
stay the same,
understanding they do not want
their beliefs challenged,
hoping their world will not change.

It's no wonder they pull at my heart,
yank on my mind,
with arms around my ankles,
clinging tight for a perfect woman
standing for generations past,
perplexed
by wisdom of my intuitive choices.

As for me . . .
I quietly breathe, *no,*
knowing I will not go on as before.
I feel it in my bones.
My breath speaks new truth,
and the sage in me again says, *yes,*
to this primal breath of knowing.

Come to Your Life

Regardless of what you think
your life should have been,
or what you have believed
could have been better choices,
or what voices said to tempt
your heart to turn and run,
regardless of what you know,
what you don't know, or
what you wish to understand—

Come to your life today
with an open, healed heart,
allow your dear soul
to reflect its deeper truth,
increase your capacity to love,
emulate your unique wisdom.
Simply come . . .
with greater appreciation
for all that has been before.

Come to your life filled,
not empty.
Wrap your arms around you.
Kneel to the mysterious calls
you hear from the gods.
Arrive at your place shouting
to the Universe to prepare
for your living an even more
exquisite version of you.

Ecstatic Liberation

As her days moved on
after her fiftieth year,
there came
in an unexpected moment—
the brilliant emergence
of an ecstatic birth.

The bursting wave
of explosive energy
filled the sweet, small bud
then rushed upward—
like widespread wings
encircling a beloved's heart.

With her mouth closed tight,
she halted her voice to silence,
intuiting others would not yet
receive what was manifesting—
preparing to birth forth into
robust, dynamic sage fullness.

It came rising from within
the deep sacred well
of her mysterious cave
of potent, pure creativity—
steeped with boldness,
bound by fierce strength.

Continue

She would wait for the
grand, heightened moment
to release her voice and
speak of those moments—
powerful creations conceived,
yet to emerge with abandon.

Could it be such a potent
brawny bursting forth
liberates copious potential—
releasing a sage's mature
genius spirit to utterly soar
on her widespread wings?

Essence

Who is this spirit
that resides in me?
What is this essence,
this inexhaustible fire
that burns throughout
my vast eternities?

What is this warmth,
this light that burned
before my father's sperm
and mother's ovum,
before my first breath,
first sight and sound?

Does this It really
remain pure, powerful
and untouched
by people, places, things
and tough miracles
of this world I came to?

Is It truly safe from
my greatest doubts
and disappointments,
fears and resentments,
and even loves that
sculpt my path in life?

Continue

Does it say It is—
my power of presence,
my power of god within,
my timeless, omnipresent
effervescence that
will not, does not, cannot—

And is not altered by
what I say, what I do,
who or what I know,
where I am, who I love?
Is it an eternal flame
sourcing essence of my life?

Fallow Time

Winter darkness comes home
deep within the stilled soul
in the quiet, cold, long nights
while the forest floor lies dormant
under the dead growth of summer.

Recall last spring's greening and
lively vibrancy that followed, and
all that withered from fall's harvest.
Now shelter your dear heart,
rest in the furry crescent of
your own warm hospitality,
breathe in arcs of light promising
to defy such eager deep darkness.

Bow to dreams, worries and wars,
disappointments, accomplishments,
and ways of being that served you—
all guides to Love's transformation.
Lay them all on glowing cinders
of earlier seasons, and silently
bless the ash that carries the
stories and teachings to heaven.

Open wide your cloak and offer
beauty of nakedness to shadows

Continue

cast by evening's flickering fire.
Stand on the hearth of pure potentiality—
empty as a flute without a melody,
clear as a mirror reflecting no thing,
bare as a page before a thought
is scribed into the written word.

Remember, the magic of Winter
is potency to impregnate new life—
seeds sourced by god's breath in
rich fallow soil of your rare essence.
Can you celebrate the dense darkness,
bless the light that will prevail, and
welcome god's gift of gestation that
nurtures its mysterious sacredness?

Winter darkness will come home
deep within your stilled soul
in the quiet, cold, long nights, and
your soul will surely soon quicken
with heartbeats of god's new life.

Finding Home

Just before the full moon that month,
she knew she would leave home to find home.
It was as if the fierce winds of December
rode in on robust clouds heading westward,
and the screen door of her house
could no longer hold back
the winds of change.

Banging and flapping shutters
snapped off their hinges
exposing unobstructed views
from windows of her frozen destiny.
Too long she had sat in front of fire
in the hearth that spit and flickered,
belching ash onto gray concrete walls
that fortressed her life.
She no longer would walk lightly
side-stepping cracks in the foundation
but ran wildly, hesitancy banished,
skimming planks in the icy porch
to catch the howling wind
as she flew into the gods' unknown.

With her gingham skirt aflame
and her innocent children in tow,

Continue

17

she followed her name whirring on ahead,
on down that country road.
She had to leave home to find home
and some day, maybe one summer day,
she may return to visit,
knock on the screen door
plastered with white cottonwood seeds,
each with a morsel of ancient wisdom
waiting for gnarly, rugged growth—
seeds, like little tough pioneers
just waiting for a ride with the gods of wind
heading west, hell bent on heaven.

And remembering her gusty ride,
I just hope that any woman who desires
to push through her own screen door
will realize sometimes we have to leave home
to find home . . .
perhaps, more than once
as we till the sod of our lifetime.

Forgotten Contentment

One sleepy eye opened.
I sighed,
peering through morning dew,
wet and beading
on a bedroom window
that frames the guardian fir tree—
the towering one,
that has been a natural companion
through years of living
on this coastal hillside.

Slowly, my other eye followed.
I squinted into the early coral dawn
bathing the Olympic Mountains.
My fingers grazed across
the warm nap of soft fleece sheets
as I became keenly aware
of an inner silence . . .
a sweet comfort,
like the quiet aftermath of
a stilled Midwest plains storm.

Perplexed, I sighed
into a stare of curiosity.
Is this my soul's quiet breathing
after years of wrangling

Continue

with that which it agreed to
before my mother's conception—
this breathing in,
breathing out,
without the ageless gnawing grip
of some thing?

Is this the pure essence
of the soul's autumn honey
that now permeates the combs
of this body, this mind,
clearing for its sweet spirit
to finally, . . . to finally
come back home to the queen's hive
of forgotten contentment?
Is this the place of love's divine warmth
before I was begotten?

And I ask the wise guardian tree,
*Is it now that I live
or, is it now that I can die?*

Freedom

Sometimes my heart hangs on
imagining a great disappointment
simply cannot be true.
It hangs on to fragments
like clenching a rope of time
stretched taunt
with just a few frail fibers
still remaining connected
amongst all the frayed ends,
not willing to see
that even one strand
has power to chain
evolution of my soul.

Sometimes it takes a long time
for the heart to move
into freedom.
Even if it has taken 1,909 days,
perhaps 164,937,600 seconds;
or if it has traveled 3,597 miles,
lived 60 years
or nearly a lifetime,
one day its fulcrum may shift,
and the advantage of hanging on
is no longer apparent,
and power of illusion
rolls up like smoke into heaven.

Continue

Sometimes in an unpredicted moment
trust will wed
the beloved surrender
and it appears that all is well . . .
and it is.
Then, the last fiber of false hope
snaps—
and the soul sighs
as we calmly remember
that freedom
can only flow
through the reality
of our heart's liberation.

Half Moon

Gazing at the night sky,
I am drawn into the half moon,
astonishingly illuminating
artistic light motifs
dancing across my bed
from some 238,857 miles
and far beyond into unknown.

Galleries of blue gray puffs
waft between us,
yet, she is constant and steady,
omnipresent
as clouds pass, reflecting splendor,
shining bright into me,
offering her wisdom.

Tonight, half not seen,
cast over by shadow,
yet, perfecting her whole,
tells story that each exists
not without the other—
shadow is as primary
as that remaining in light.

What if we only believed?
What if we were confident

Continue

23

that our own shadow
consecrated our humanness?
What if we welcomed its secrets
waiting to be known as
fundamental to our wholeness?

As surely as strait waters
must ebb and flow,
as the tide rises and falls,
and waves roll in and out
by her mysterious power,
she will return again and again
teaching the truth of life.

Will we learn to resist
turning over in our beds
with backs to her teachings,
closing our eyes to a wall
and refuse to shrink
from the magnificence
of our own mysterious shadow?

Watch.
Listen.
She compassionately urges
the truth of our lives—
the necessity of dark and light,
by the enchanting nature of
her glorious half moon.

Home

Come
to that
which longs
for you
to be fully home
to all
that you are.

Your home
awaits
with open doors,
the threshold flush;
you
need not
stumble in.

House of Faith

Tell me how
to be at home
with faith.

I know what love is like—
that exhilarating freedom to
soar in tandem with another,
careening through
every room of the heart.

And joy—
the rise of enlivening
contagious amusement,
felicity, and bliss that
fills the rafters of the soul.

Even hope—
eternal longing that lives
in mind's hearth, fanning flames
that whatever will somehow,
someday be different.

Of course, gratitude—
singing in various verses
of abundant well-being,
is always ready to echo
through chambers of my heart.

But faith—
how do I know It
for which god awakens me
in my bed and whispers,
It is all about faith.

When will faith pass over
my soil and notice the
river rocks in my path?
What will it take to come
to my weathered door?

So faith, . . . I say,
Just bolt right on in
and don't you even dare
hide in old dusty closets
or dim corners in the hall.

Come to my dining table.
Heap your overflowing
cornucopia in bowls and plates.
Sit and eat with me,
you and I, dear faith.

I will welcome you
like a long lost friend—
this time we will not sleep

Continue

but become dazed and drunk
on aged wine of bold trust.

Then after morning comes,
you will reside with me
and I will reside with you—
yes, we will co-abide
together in my house of faith.

And gratefully,
you will be at home with me,
dear faith.

Lover of Unearthing

I feel unearthed,
like strong, tall fir trees
withstanding years
of vigorous winter weather—
suddenly with too much,
winds too severe,
deeply penetrating rains,
cloaks of snow too heavy
to possibly withstand
all that comes at once.

And, in a moment
of imminent cosmic timing,
roots heave, tumble up,
liberate interwoven girding,
expose magnificent rocks
releasing sweet fragrance
of rich and fertile soil.
And there, trees fall—
welcomed by the longing
Lover of Unearthing.

Exhaling into uncertainty
of having conceived
the advent of nursing logs
in the cool, soft bed

Continue

29

of the embracing forest,
there comes the absolute
necessity to surrender life
as before here lived
into an alluring, satisfying,
resonating cosmic sigh.

Comes understanding
there is nothing at all
that trees can do
to possibly hold back
the elements of change.
Nothing at all.
Nothing, but readiness,
willingness to be welcomed
by the Beloved
Lover of Unearthing.

I, too, lay on the damp
fertile winter forest floor
of my life,
asking for readiness—
willingness to receive
the great cosmic Beloved,
to conjoin in co-creating
birth of authenticity.
Finally, . . . I reach for
my *Lover of Unearthing.*

The Sage's Menses

In her night dream
when it seemed impossible,
a stunning menses came—
the shedding of what is not needed,
the cleansing of what no longer serves,
the leaving of what cannot go with her,
in preparation for an amazing new creation:
her unfolding sacred path embodying her sage,
her yet unlived story.

It was the sage's menses—
astounding,
brilliant,
red,
grounded,
preparing for
her yet untold story.

Winter's Light

This Winter's day,
I know not
my unfolding path in Spring,
yet I trust a sense of hibernating
with the Mother of Spring's creation.

Like tall Douglas firs,
I wait . . .
believing that Spring waits,
wanting to breathe pregnant air again . . .
reaching to the heavens
in mysterious, amazing ways,
up from wet, generative land
where we both dream
to burst forth new branches.

I believe,
like in the floors of the forest,
muted earthy hues
in the floors of my living
will once again transform
into the vibrant richness
that only happens by sun's light
rising from Winter's day
cast on Spring's awakening.

Dare I choose to trust
the wisdom of Winter's light
gently urging
awaking from hibernation?
Dare I open my heart
to its rhythmic invitation—
to be changed by a luminosity
that gently seeks birth
in my life?

Wonders of Wind & Sun

She tilted her head into the wind
through a dirty backdoor window—
her glistening hair streamed back
whipping up, down, here and there,
her eyes nearly closed with tiny slits
barely visible in the ruckus of air,
pleasure and contentment radiating
on her lovely, delicate young face,
completely immersed in summer sun.

I wondered . . .

What if occasionally
we simply climbed into the backseat
of the king cab of our life—
the past invisible in a rearview mirror,
the future not yet even thought of,
fully, completely,
acquiescing to the wild,
captivating goodness of *now,*
fevered with delight in solar breath?

I wondered . . .

Wouldn't we be exquisitely enlivened?
What more than to travel with the gods
of wind and sun, ushering us into
infatuating whimsies of abundant joy,
desiring to fuel more moments of bliss?
Yes, imagine spirit guides riding along
in the backseat of our daily lives,
arousing us into such simple caprice,
captivating us in absolute contentment—

Immersing us in wonders of wind and sun.

Fire in the Well

✿

Chapter II

Fire of Passion

invites us to live passionately in the moment,
to foster love, joy, wonder and gratitude,
to deepen pleasures in our living,
and
to make vital, life-affirming choices.

Awakening

When you awaken in the morning,
don't moan that the clock shines 5 a.m.,
or begrudge disturbance of the wind with rain
howling through the open window,
or ask what the day can do for you.
Awaken asking,
"What makes me come alive?"
"Where is my passion?"

What arouses your heart even more than
waking to a dance of first light shimmering on water—
or savoring sweet sounds of a grandchild's slumber?
Possibly, your heart stirs considering women
who don't have a safe place to sleep.
Perhaps, it is that a woman can now marry a woman.
Maybe it's that idea deep inside that wants to be seen,
and whispers, *You can do whatever you imagine.*

Allow things that stir you to enter your heart.
Breathe freely.
Feel life flowing through your body,
through your being.
What do you love?
What cause tugs at your heart?
What makes you want to celebrate?
What art needs you?

A wise woman opens her eyes in morning
and invites that which desires to live through her,
steadfastly understanding the same power
Hildegard, Theresa, Jesus,
Buddha and QuanYin used
is also in her.
She passionately welcomes her day
in relationship with, and as a co-creator of, life.

Boundless Love

In the sunroom
of an Alzheimer's wing,
seasoned souls gathered.
My eyes searched for her,
and then,
I saw her crumpled body
swaying like a rag doll
suspended
by a strap around her belly,
barely shuffling
one foot
and
then the other,
struggling to keep her chin up
off her one flat, elongated breast.

A woman sang,
her harsh voice echoing loudly.
One clapped hands over her ears
in perfect rhythm,
as shameless demands fell aimlessly
from longing mouths
into the circle of wheel chairs.
I watched an old man shuffle in
to visit his beloved, then reach

awkwardly across her twisted body
crumpled in an outstretched lounger
and tenderly caress her parted lips.
Her eyes remained fixed on the ceiling,
as a slight upturn appeared
at the corners of her mouth.

I walked to her,
took my aunt's soft chin
in the palms of my hands.
Leaning close, I kissed her forehead,
hoping to leave an imprint
of my lipstick forever
on this woman
who had believed in me
all my life.
I breathed out, *I'll love you forever.*
Opening her eyes,
looking up into my face,
she faintly smiled
and whispered,
And the same for you, my dear.

Could it be this is *boundless love*—
no limits,
nor constraints,

Continue

41

or way that life restrains its power?
Is it through this power of love
that our soul speaks messages
during long moments of silence,
messages that sustain us
after we hesitantly
gather our things
and leave
for the very last time?
Is it boundless love that
carries us on with another
forever tucked in our soul?

Elder Love

She waits yet again for music
of that sweet, strong voice,
and the rise, that comes from
she can't even imagine where,
embodying a sensation
of having no legs
while the belly swirls
with confusion
as to whether it is ill, or
if it is wild, ancient longing
breaking forth
in a surge of passion,
jarred . . .
like a gasket lid
screwed down tight
on an engorged heart,
that dares conjure living in love,
even so, after so many years.

Reminisce, dear love,
seeing in your mind's eye
swirling juxtaposing angles
of a dusty wood ceiling
in a third story wing,
while heat of a summer
longs to still be that summer,
wondering,

Continue

Is it now fall, or is it winter?
Love doesn't even care—
does not matter
come spring,
summer,
fall,
or pending winter.
Loving touch is soul's manna,
and roaming caresses ache to
birth love itself once more.

For this,
old hearts dare splatter open
to be owned by passion
once again
after so many infertile years.

Emergence of Passion

She was lopped across
a dark green, overstuffed couch.
Her black lace bra strap
draped a porcelain shoulder
suggesting hints of sexual fantasy
smoldering in a lovely cleavage—
certainly not to be veiled by a
cashmere leopard pullover or
the tight pursing of tawny lips.

Through the windowpane,
hazy sunlight crowned her red hair
and shone on her etched face.
She wrestled with discernment—
reaching a decision to not pursue
lurking potential for a torrid affair
with palpable, untethered desire
that her heart and body craved,
and her quick mind rationalized.

It had been a sudden, steamy
eruption of longing and passion.
A door opened when someone
from long ago broke the silence.
Her heart opened wide, and
unapologetically exposed that

Continue

which had been raw, forgotten,
ambushing desire—
hunting her like a hungry panther.

She was sixty-six years old,
'for god's sake,' she cried
with quick cultural self-judgment.
Where to take such intensity . . .
dormant and obscured by the
mundane rote aspects of life
and a parallel, lackluster dance
with a dependable husband
of over forty some odd years?

Agony was kind, however,
to reveal her buried longing.
The emergence of passion
surfaced without expectancy,
flushing through every cell,
leaving piercing eyes soft,
teaching authentic self-love
and fierce, bodily-knowing
previously in silent slumber.

Hers was an exemplary life,
predictable roles well-defined.
Then she seemed to implode,
discovering ancient potential
that offered compassionate gifts—

self-love, wisdom and grace,
igniting fiery healing with
creative fervor that demanded
honor of greater expression.

Let us lower our eyebrows
and pray no woman leave
without asking how she might
embrace inexplicable, fertile,
underlying womanly passion,
hold its emergence gently
and lovingly fall into arms
of her own lush sageness
birthed in mystifying ways.

Just take a moment now,
and lower your eyebrows.
Pray without judgment
that no woman leave her life
without honestly asking
how she might creatively
hold emergence of passion,
gently honor its mystery, and
wield its power for greatness.

Endless Passion of Now

Coffee cup lowered from my creased lips,
I take the love letters from the closet
noticing my heart is still…
perhaps, still quietly roused.
As I pull my warm, purple shawl
around these sagging shoulders
I suddenly feel a ghost of the embrace
of this one particular old lover.
I desperately try to conjure vignettes
smoldering from past years of my life,
like tired little dancers stuck in time
behind drawn velvet stage drapes,
dreaming of one more irresistible moment
consumed by love's illusive passion.
Yet, the past is a narrow opening in the mind
with no way back to its beginning.
Knitting my grayed eyebrows,
old, timeworn memories tease me.
Maybe there is still time
to be owned by love again—
that crazy essence that takes everything,
and sometimes gives nothing.
I notice a lump welling in my throat,
my chest feeling full,
my eyes moist with salty memories.
Breathing out a melancholy sigh,

I reluctantly snap from illusion
suddenly savoring the aroma
of this fresh-brewed coffee while
wiping pink lipstick off the morning cup.
I tuck the bunch of tattered-edges
under my arm, and shuffle to the porch.
I sway leaning back, grabbing the arm
of the white wicker swing.
Simple beauty of the early sun rising in fog
begins to flirt with my senses.
Sparkling dew drops in an autumn web
at the upper corner of the porch
interrupt my thoughts.
I realize the truth.
I am content with longing or no longing,
with resting in the endless passion
of this precious moment…this now,
realizing love no longer chains my heart.
I tilt my head back, lifting my old face
toward the heat breaking through trees,
realizing—
really, it is late.
I feel the sea breeze toss my white thin hair,
then watch the soft folded papers lift up
off the pink flowered cushion.
I smile, slowly swinging,
seeing them all flitter into the distance.
Ah….yes, love has set me free.
I take another sip of my morning coffee
and toss my toast to the birds.

Faces of Eternity

Through a fog of rapid living
during so many decades
comes a welcomed quiet, . . .
yet, old disquieted memories
find a way to enter my heart.

Who are these dear images
emerging from long ago,
with innocent, intense eyes
that once seeded dreams in
a younger woman I once was?

Who are they after all this time?
Are they imps with simple curiosity
arising from tiny, treasured places
as I recall choices I did not make,
choices I did, paths taken and not?

These inquiring voices will not
be silenced—as if I even would.
I ask, *Are we imbued in eternity,*
having come together before,
and perhaps yet to circle again?

Maybe it's an enduring desire
of five billion years, or so—
timeless sojourners deepening
in the Omnipresent Mystery . . .
having once known pure joy,

Returning, reaching out once again,
like hesitant fingers touching
dots of delicate autumn dew
on the eternal face of a beloved,
simply not wanting to go away.

Ghost of Love

The moment I first saw you
I knew you knew me.
You knocked on the door
of my soul and I let you in.
You were like a part of me
reaching back to a place
I had forgotten,
reaching back to a place
I hadn't remembered,
a place where I had learned
the truth about coming alive,
yet left behind in earlier time.

It was your gaze into my soul,
your embrace and love,
your unfailing belief in me
that was luscious balm
for my tender heart.
It was there
I discovered faith,
like a young child at sea
finally discovering a safe harbor—
that sweet resting place
where storms would not deter
the sweet purity of life.

That bit of Universe time—
a time for us,

graced dear love,
then pierced with deep grief as
I watched your ship leave my harbor,
gliding away on the seas
one winter morning.
I watched as the beauty of you
grew smaller in the distance,
as the swells of life rose and fell
until the fading horizon
welcomed you into her arms.

The harbor that was ours
was where I learned about truth,
where I learned that
the winds of love could
steady my mast,
a wind I trusted to anchor my life.
Yet, the winds of change
and rumbling bore tides
can also tear a mast to shreds,
unknot tight sturdy ties,
its trade can set opposing sails,
and hurl about a precious life.

So, as it comes to pass,
I occasionally open the hull
in my mind to see
if you are still there,
and what I see
is a ghost of love—
one that smiles tenderly,

Continue

one that reaches to touch
edges of my damp cheeks.
And, when I reach for you,
I only feel a touch of cool sea air
press ever so gently into me.

Then, hesitantly, I turn away
still grateful
still thankful
for learning how to love well;
still grateful
still thankful
for the teacher who gave me life.

Grand Love

She was 92.
Her beloved was 88.
They warmed me
like few lovers have.
Their tenderness,
respect
and gratitude
prevailed throughout
their late season days.
And only like
old sweethearts can,
they always discovered
satisfying ways
to express steadfast,
tender love;
to share gems
of intimacy
that come with time,
and grace hearts
with fulfillment.

Growing older
day by day,
they beheld each other
with grand love,
a mystery
nothing could deter.

Continue

Although years claimed
their harsh mark
in many unfriendly,
unkind ways,
gazing into each other's
wise eyes,
holding each other's
feeble hands,
truly dismissed
any naive notion
that seasoned love
could possibly belong
to man and woman
of their youth.

The world yearns
for what they shared,
like writing
I love you
on plaid, flannel backs
in the night,
stroking white hair
with gnarled fingers,
blowing kisses
through windowpanes,
eyes twinkling
with mischievous,
ancient laughter.
Their endearment
was not for taking
but to be witnessed

as they continued
their art of forgiveness,
their joy of being
dearly loved.

They knew their breath
was precious life,
and did not allow
a loving moment
to escape
their few fragile days.
They engaged
soulful pleasures,
ever imbued
by simple delights.
And, like old lovers
with new eyes,
they gazed tenderly
under drooping lids
into windows
of each other's
dear soul,
treasuring grand love—
their legacy
of love's sweet mystery.

Love's Tough Miracle

Whether we quarrel with love,
wrangle with human limitations
or perhaps misunderstand god,
there are times each of us
must travel a solitary path
until we are humbled
by love's tough miracle
teaching us what aspects
of ourselves are separated from
the true nature of who we are.

I have heard that fiery courage
unleashed by the soul's sage
just may spark burning down walls
of an invincible armored heart,
gaining entry to all those pieces
that long for union once again.
I hear that after she has her way,
it is the Queen Sage who kisses
the back of our hands,
and quietly, patiently, waits.

Could it be . . .
in such moments of time
it was my soul's sage that
unleashed love's tough miracle,

set me on fire,
dismantled my invincible heart
and taught me
to lovingly gather
the cinders of my life into
the blessed journey of *I am?*

My heart ponders the query,
as I notice a moist lip imprint
on the back of my hands,
like dew on autumn roses.
Is it the sage's invitation,
a wise cairn,
inviting another way,
changing my life forever,
blessing me
by love's tough miracle?

Lovers of the Sea

Lovers emerged from the sea
and laid on the cool beach
in driftwood last night—
embellishing the shore
with red roses and aged shells,
mingling sand with sea.

Fragrant remnants of flora
graced the altar of those
intoxicated by passion—
no doubt the sweet taste of lips
and longing bodies
marked the evening cloth.

Save muse and delight
that love's desire abided there,
where wild roses tangle and bloom—
there where lovers entangled
on the moonlit beach
as their heat ascended to heaven.

Dare we look under our years,
recall what we passionately dreamt
then step onto ancient sand
with our sweet desire in hand, and
surrender to magic of the sea again
one latter summer night.

Magnificence of Life

I have tasted
magnificence of life
for which
I have not words . . . .
rendered voiceless,
wordless—

Wordless,
like an unborn child
not knowing
how to possibly describe
marvel of its existence,
a spectacular gem
nestled in a corner
of It's mysterious
womb of life.

Simply,
voiceless,
wordless

Ah, wise
seasoned sage,
savor magnificence
of your life
for which
you have not words.

Continue

Speechless,
like a newborn child
not knowing
how to possibly express
marvel of your existence,
yet understand that
your essence is
your gem,
your wealth.

Simply,
voiceless,
wordless

Savor this moment,
honor yourself,
and
the magnificence
of your precious life
in this world.

My Anchor

I am captured by the sea's spirit,
taken by her immensity,
enticed by mysteries of worlds
hidden below rising and falling
of her elegant cadence,
of wild stirrings,
of creations only imagined.

I come to her shores for strength,
to cast my cares,
to touch drops of understanding,
to believe I am one with greatness.
I feel the soothing heartbeat
of her rhythmic waves
slowly calm my racing mind.

Squinting my eyes in awe,
I walk meditatively beside her
clearing my thoughts,
buoying my spirits
as she fills the well of my soul,
as I sigh into sweet release,
as I breathe in salty inspiration.

She opens a portal of wisdom
releasing a blessing of insights,

Continue

drawing me away from
misguided ways
of my darting mind,
of an unsettled heart,
of cast-away dreams.

I go to her seeking a feeling
of connection with god,
listening for even one word—
a message that I need
to let go of regrets,
to believe in the unknown,
to live life passionately.

I love her.
And, in her presence
I anchor my life.

Night in Ouray

Huge delicate snowflakes
drifted to earth
on a cold, black night in Ouray;
lovely, as each crystal
floated to its destiny of union—
down from the heavens
through sheered rock mountains
alive with wild tapestry of timeless life.

Cool lightness of snow
caressed my steaming face,
intense heat of hot springs
soothed my welcoming body,
as I utterly surrendered as one
with nature's holy Beloved,
elating my senses
with quiet, tantalizing grandeur.

Intricate gems mystically penetrated
my anticipation
as I settled into
hot medicinal waters of Earth—
up from the roiling
salty heat of Her secret caves,
as She held witness to my awe
of such aromatic darkness.

Continue

I laid in Her rich womb
of eternal offerings wondering,
Am I this impermanent snow
and all that is in the snow?
Am I the mineral springs and
each intricate element therein?
Am I the steam, the mountains?
Might I be sweet dark of night?

My heart opened to Her mystery—
I am She, and She is me.
I am you, you are me.
All is part of us,
as we are part of It.
We are separate,
yet, we are not.
We are the dance of life.

The dance that joins us,
melding our hearts
with a song of universal oneness
that echoes through the
great inclusive heart of humanity,
pulsing with peace and tranquility,
shone in magical moments gifted
as this intimate night in Ouray.

One Thing

One thing I must say,
You are my Beloved—
and I know not why
the gods smiled on me
generously gifting
this everlasting fire
in my belly of being.

One thing I will tell,
You are my heart's manna—
inimitably nourishing love
which cannot flourish in
the absence of our souls
converging in this journey
through immortal time.

One thing I whisper,
You are my deep passion—
so come, I welcome you
to my innermost hearth
which is fomented by
the Divine wind of
our life-giving breath.

Continue

One thing I give you,
I give you me—
I stand before you
without pretense,
my tender story naked,
humbly knowing this
is all I have to give.

Sacred Thirst

Oh, sacred thirst—
the familiar, unfulfilled longing
that entraps the heart.
Once satisfied,
it relishes cherished content
and revels
in magnificent fulfillment
of what is hoped to be eternal.

And then slowly,
the quenched desire dissipates
into quiet gnawing once again
at the corners of lips,
in the recesses of the heart,
as the satisfying glory melts
into the embrace of thirst
for one more delicious goblet
poured full at the table
of the dear beloved.

Then again,
the brave heart relinquishes itself
to an ever-magnificent contentment,
though it will most certainly
fall in love again with longing—
like sweetness that desires
to infuse late harvested grapes
for sacred wine of the goddesses.

Salt

I stepped onto the sand
at nearly sunset,
sighing into a gentle breeze
that carried the gift of salt—
caressing my face,
invigorating my lungs,
enlivening my senses,
preserving evening with
absolute cathartic magic.

Gazing across the sea,
piquant salt of lovers
rushed into my memory,
shaking my heart
with tender, zesty emotions
of a time when life
was pregnant with life
and nothing mattered
but the sweat of loving.

In remembering . . .
warm crystalline tears
fell slowly, gently
over my cool cheeks
making broad turns
over the bow of my lip,

seeping salt onto my tongue,
as I stood silently in awe
of its mysterious nature.

What if salt's teaching
is to consciously savor
it's gifts that beckon
abundant love of life—
embracing earthiness,
seasoning new horizons,
inspiring gusto for
a spicy, flavorful life until
our last and final taste?

Did I hear the sea whisper,
Yes!, with its invisible breath?
Is this the teaching for
the sage's salt-infused life—
love life,
embrace earthiness,
season new horizons,
inspire gusto
for a spicy, flavorful life—

Until my . . .
or your . . .
last and final taste?

Story of Intimacy

I yearn
to live a story of intimacy,
beyond my youth,
beyond mid-life,
beyond society's meaning.
I desire to be deeply known,
yet fear being known
both at the same time.
It is my profound need,
like food to eat,
water to drink,
air to breathe.

I reach for waiting arms
of deep intimacy.
At times I touch its sweetness
while thinking,
I may keep secrets my own.
Yet, the voice of intimacy
asks me to share
tender stories of my heart,
of my mind,
of my soul,
share them with another
imperfect human being—

Allow another to discover
what moves me, inspires me,
drives me, hurts me,
makes me smile and sigh,
what I am running toward
and running from,
what I whisper to the gods at night,
and what silent, impish enemies
still reside deep within,
what wildness I harbor,
and what wonderful dreams
still wait deep in my heart.

What is your story?
Do you have a deep need
to be known—
to be discovered,
and re-discovered
over and over in a lifetime?
If you do, take my hand
and don't go away—
I promise to not turn from you
and perhaps, dear one,
together we will discover
a new story of intimacy.

Summer's Evening Geese

Every summer evening
at about 9:15
I hear them
summoning each other,
gathering over the ridge
at Buck Lake.
Then, with a grand swoosh
and whir,
they split air
honking and squawking,
taking flight
in perfect alignment.

They barely clear tips
of high evergreens,
spanning long
like whittled straight arrows,
leaning into that
which calls them—
Westward they go,
into coral hues,
cast by the sun resting
in the lap
of the corrugated
Olympic Mountains.

Wouldn't it be exhilarating
if at end of day,
without excuses or
halting diversions,
we simply let go . . .
lifted our hands high
and, without questions
or hesitancy,
we exuberantly proclaimed
our place
in oneness
with all living things?

Wouldn't it be exhilarating
if we aligned our intentions,
our wishes,
cleared all
that could possibly
stand in our way, and
surrendered to the drawing
tide that calls forth
an irresistible,
instinctual,
evening rampage of
raucous gratitude?

Fire in the Well

❁

Chapter III

Fire of Compassion

stirs us to practice loving kindness,
to live into the flow of loss, grief and change,
to graciously give and receive care,
and
to move through life transitions confidently.

Autumn Is Gone

I raise the window shade
and clearly see,
autumn is gone, and
winter has come.

After a dense, dark night,
I gaze across the Hood Canal,
rumpled pajamas hanging
on my still tired body.
My weathered toes curl
into the fiber of the carpet
nailed to the cool, wood floor
as I squint at Canadian geese
in perfect, sweeping formation
across a majestic silhouette.

I sigh, captured by the beauty
of the Olympic mountains
now snowcapped this morning.
I wince for the weary grass
cloaked in crisp white crystals
for the first time this season.
Heavy grayness hovers over
the water in the ebbing canal,
yet it is artistically rimmed
in a soothing hazy pink.

Running my fingers through
my eschewed hair, I wonder,
Can I still love my life?
Can I find treasures in winter,
knowing with raw respect that
She has now claimed Her season?
Standing silently in my bedroom,
I welcome Her husky voice,
and pray my soul be content
during my own late season.

I hold my arms around me
as I feel it in my bones . . .
indeed, my autumn is gone
and winter grace has come.

Bits and Bones

Blessed be those who toil
gathering bits and bones
after love lavishly had its day.
After death, the heart rummages
to satisfy unspeakable emptiness
searching with persistent queries,
wondering,

Was it some god's jester
with a cruel sense of humor,
or a trickster
scampering across the landscape
of one's life
cackling
in mischievous mockery?

Heart tucks itself under
so as to barely risk
a chance to grow,
daring the arduous pilgrimage
to imagine eyes of love again—
as if true feelings would not
survive any quirky possibility.

However, the beautiful irony
of laying down bits and bones
is that burdens begin to gently lift
and, then sometimes
self-love just may have a chance
to pierce the haunted heart
and set it free.

Day Break

Early light dares pierce tight
closed openings of my tired eyes.
I hear ground squirrels chatter,
racing back and forth across
boards foliaged in pink clematis,
while robins celebrate morning—
bopping up . . . down . . . as they do
in exuberant, tenacious staccato.

Is it truly a new dawning, though
I fear yet dreaming in night?
Could it be that cool, sweet salt
of evening's air prayerfully swept
over the warmth of my dark cover
empathically christening this day?
Could it be in one dogged moment
daybreak's light bid sorrow farewell?

And, could it be this day break
compassionately
entreats sweet living again?

Great Masters

As surely as . . .

Brown eight-eyed orb weavers
float another silk line
to the October winds,

And

Little purple and white crocus
hardily push through winter's snow
as promise of new life,

Great blue heron will arrive
at woodland nesting grounds
spring after spring—

And

I will pause a summertime eve
recalling bittersweet
and tender farewells in winter.

As surely as . . .

Great masters keenly practice
nature's seasons calling for another
web, blossom, and twig—

I will offer gratitude for each
tender memory that desires
renewal in my heart,

Season after season.

bodies stretched long and lean,
we fly toward fields flourishing
with abundant harvests,
beyond the beyond,
heavens welcoming our soar
into another intuitive unknown.

Yes, you can count on me.
I will stay with you until,
like crimson-crowned cranes
called to dances
in other fertile fields,
either you . . .
or I . . .
take flight from this place
to another land—
the heartland of our souls.

I Want To Know

I want to know
what sustains you
from the inside out
when your gut twists,
rolls and wrenches
from unmistakable taste
of sour injustice,
or when love turns its back,
or when your dad dies.

I really want to know
what gives you hope,
what gives you joy
when all else crumbles
down around your socks,
as if your life were leftovers
disintegrating to crumbs
swept off your table
right before your eyes.

What keeps you from
running for cover,
hiding under the eaves
of your otherwise
good-looking life,
when claps of thunder

Continue

or heavy, humid smell
of an impending storm
looms in your bones?

Tell me about what
ignites juicy desire
in your soul once again,
what strikes a flame that
bursts forth your "*Yes!*"
your passionate songs,
blazes with inspiration,
helps you hit high C . . .
with your heart unzipped.

What makes you tilt
your gleaming face and
throw happy hands
up to the radiant sun,
topless and barefoot—
even if the neighbors,
your dearest friends,
or perhaps your kids,
think you've turned crazy?

I just want to know.

Letting Go

As evening came in her latter years,
her heart wrangled with letting go—
letting go of possessions,
ideals of health, infinite independence,
and life itself.

Letting go of dreams
incomplete, unfinished,
that escaped from her fragile reality—
replacing desires with mustered hope
of just one more day doing what she loved.

She nestled in the comfort and safety
of her rocking chair in a quiet living room,
wisely surrendering
to honest gratefulness,
to fulfillment in reminiscing joy.

With soft smiles on her thin lips,
she gazed tenderly into faces of those she loved
while struggling to let go,
still wanting to hold on,
yet surrendering to the evening of her life.

Magdalena

It took a long time…
a very long time
to finally jump off the ship
freighted with spoon-fed theology
and mindless doctrines.
I told the captain of patriarchy,
the man of vengeance and judgment,
I had to find a god who looked like me.
If I was going to wrangle with life,
I wanted one of those
busty, voluptuous wooden women
nailed to the front of ships
to save me—
I wanted one of those
weathered, courageous females
who unflinchingly
presses into unpredictable storms
with her long, painted wood skirts
whipped back in the wild gale.
I wanted one of those
beautiful carved figureheads
to come alive,
to come to my rescue,
to hold me in her strong arms,
let me rest between her broad knees
as I shed tears in her buxom breasts,
take my hand with her sturdy grasp
and ride with me on the seas

confidently
while together we navigated
toward the harbor
of the Divine Feminine
shining bright Her beacon
across the rambunctious swells,
until we heard Her voice
shouting out, *"Come! Here I am!*
Your Magdalena!
I will give you shelter.
I will give you peace.
I will give you wisdom.
Welcome home
to a god who looks like you!"

Motherless

Dazed, I yanked a jacket
from the cloak closet,
stepped out on the porch
in the early morning fog.
I welcomed the touch
of heavy mist
on my face
as I walked and wondered,
How will my life
be different
without her here?

How can a daughter
ever be ready
to return
to her first home,
motherless—
no Mother waiting,
watching,
with loving, green eyes,
nor welcoming smile
on a sweet, anticipating face
etched with maternal love?

I wondered,
Who teaches children
to live life
motherless?

Quiet Compassion

Faintly, in a far distance,
silenced heart-wrenching cries
of a forgotten young woman
can once again be heard.
She, whose eager womb and blood
containing cherished dreams
washed away life essence
that could not stay
for her longing heart
to immerse in maternal love,
once again hears heart's muffled cry.

Primordial anguish quickens
deep, loving compassion
in recalling stifled screams
so visceral and penetrating
that the universe trembled—
instantly shattering life,
while helpless,
furrowed brows
could feel the palpable and
welcoming cool breath
of death's hovering angels.

Continue

Now, she tenderly touches
the one faded knife line,
once naval to pubis,
as quiet compassion erupts,
honoring the solitary mark
remaining for the world
to reverence ancient sorrow,
once inconceivable
for black-cloaked celibates
who fidgeted with prayer beads
and tinkling silver chains.

Blessed are women's bodies
who are keepers of barren stories.
Blessed are fresh, old tears
that flow over buried memories
of naïve, dormant, dense grief.
Blessed are the dreamt-of
fetal souls who briefly merged
then chose other paths,
leaving behind aged remnants,
now fertile . . .
to birth tender, quiet compassion.

Sacred Friend

When I stand in the
middle of the fire,
will you come near and
stand by my side?
Will you dare hold
my hand in yours?

When I wrangle with
the fire's wisdom, and
perhaps question god,
will you look directly into
reflections in my eyes
and see Her perfection?

When I am humbled by
miracles of heat teaching
that as ice becomes water,
fire also changes form,
will you trust the truth
of who I am becoming?

When I am consumed
by hungry, wild flames,
will you remain with me,
wipe sweat from my brow,

Continue

and eagerly applaud my
expanding transformation?

Will you be a sacred friend,
encourage me to live *me,*
celebrate my new incarnation—
knowing my Divine spark
certainly can no more die . . .
than god can.

She Left

In dimness of the room,
fragrant with flowers,
her brow furrowed
while dry tears fell.
She muttered utterances,
no doubt attempting
to remain with what
she knew had been real.

It's okay, I assured us.
Nothing more,
no reason to worry,
nor need to fear.
Her angels gathered,
patient for her surrender;
Divine Mother waited,
with hands outstretched.

I whispered to her,
*Return to arms of your
first and last Mother—
Her soft, cool retreat
awaits your lovely,
beautiful, vibrant soul.*

Continue

Slowly her eyes opened,
and she moaned, *Damn.*

Two mornings later,
cancer won, and she left.
Sweet Mother of Heaven,
she left—
from body to iridescent light
as whiff of the angels gathered,
taking part of me with her,
leaving part of her with me.

Silence

Silence follows . . .

A poet's last word of the poem,
a runner's last step in a marathon,
a lover's last touch after lovemaking,
a beloved's last blink from deep gaze,
a friend's last breath before death.

In moments, days . . . or more—
the body surrenders into quiet inertness,
the tongue fills the mouth with no words,
the eyes close locking treasured memories,
the ears only hear heart's perpetual rhythm.

Silence invites us . . .

To draw balm of gratefulness
from her ample breasts . . .
until another word, another step,
touch, gaze, or breath,
captures us again in the sea of sweet living.

While silence rests, comes wonder:
what if we once again yield,
trust the tender call,
when the Divine beckons us
to once more be held by the mystery

Of the silence . . . that follows.

This I Know

This I know for certain—
love is tough.
Love's potency is nearly indestructible.
It is patient and sustains
with hopeful openheartedness.

I know love does not give up easily.
Yet, when it does
it surrenders exhausted,
emptying exhalation
without in-breath.

Knowing intolerable aridity,
love may give way,
settle face down
into long, thin grooves
in one's heart—

And there, . . . dissipate,
day by day,
into dry,
impermeable
lifelessness.

I know love appears to surrender
to completion.
Yet, when it does
something other than love
has seeped into cracks of the heart—

Distorting its essence,
warping its beauty.
And, love knows
that
does not belong to itself.

Then god paces softly.
She moistens love's soul
with Her tears,
and becomes
a lover with fallow time.

This I know.

Valleys of Betrayal

Exhaling awe from my heart
into red haze of early morning,
I gaze into valleys and canyons
from a vista of Hawaii's Waimea.
I am struck by what seems like
nature's harsh intentional will—
gargantuan gaps severing
the magnificent island
with an enduring gash
wielded by profound power,
separating west from east . . .
all the way to Southern Shore.

Raw layers in steep red cliffs
expose ancient tissue of Kaua'i.
Isolated spires rise from canyons
as if to attempt union after separation.
Yet, life clearly moves on, evidenced
by carpets of green vegetative heather,
graced by hovering little white storks.
These vast mysteries invite queries
about the nature of betrayal—
irreparable acts creating separation,
like nature acting against herself,
or humanity colluding against nature.

Have you ever been astonished
by your own ability to deploy
irretrievable, irreversible power—
hurtful words that punch holes
in someone's unsuspecting heart,
your capacity to deceive another
or to embellish fragile stories
undermining the belly of friendship;
perhaps, fallout from courting
short-sighted self-preservation
leaving ginormous rifts, gullies,
dividing one from another?

We may even be burdened by
trails of betrayal our ancestors left
or, no doubt more profound,
unconscious or conscious betrayal
of our own authentic personal truth,
until one day we wake up to
the bitter sweetness of self-honesty.
As our haze of infallibility lifts,
what choices do we consider
to evade valleys of betrayal,
to re-connect isolated spires
in the arid valleys of our heart?

What choices do we have when
we see storks offering new life,
patiently circling over our head?

Continue

103

Maybe it takes wisdom of a sage
to see all things gift us with chances
to discover what really matters,
to live into living compassionately,
to be wiser in righting upheavals
in the landscape of relationships
through the power of sincere love,
through healing with forgiveness,
betwixt craggy valleys of betrayal.

Voice of God

I think I am hearing the voice of god,
and my ears are filled with It.
Resonating *Abwoon* floats into the dome
of my sanctuary
like the ancient call of a barred owl,
wings spanned wide,
rising from the earth to its well-lit perch
on a far-up branch of the evergreen.

I feel the gauzy wind of *Abwoon!*
stir through me, enfold me,
pause . . . ,
encircle pools of my closed eyes.
I sense its gossamer, ethereal vibrations
rush in subtle ripples through my body,
touch deep, minute places in my soul,
then rise to its peak in reverent cadence.

Abwoon compassionately holds me,
and in brief stillness of resting breath,
I wonder if It desires to hear me sing?
Am I singing It, or is It singing me?
Can it be just my voice,
or need it be many voices
that create heavenly sounds of god?
Abwoon d'bwashmaya, sing through me!

Wilderness

I feel nothing.
After years of feeling so many things,
I touch the mirror and wonder,
Who am I becoming?
Strangely, I feel silence.

I walk along the sea's shore
and gaze into summer's night.
I sit in my den and listen for god.
I share love and practice kindness.
How can I not feel beyond this quiet?

Have I been banished from
imaginations, dreams, and passion
that previously inspirited my life?
Can I not conjure up some thing
that entreats my heart not to sleep?

Lowering lids and graying temples
remind me of lessening time as
I wonder if this is sane—
a freakish cleansing of my spirit
before the last sprint of my journey?

Is this . . . *wilderness?*
Am I engulfed in a Divine ambush
that begs me to rest in the backwoods
of my soul and wait for the
truest of my nature to quicken?

Does this wilderness know
what I will leave behind . . . .
what I will claim as my own?
Does this wilderness really
know my name?

Fire in the Well

❀

Chapter IV

Fire of Vision

calls us to create a living legacy
that supports greater good,
to manifest deeper fulfillment,
to impart a wise, mentoring spirit, and
to honor intergenerational connectedness.

A River Through My Life

Remember, my child

You are a river through my life.
I feel you coming through me.
I marvel at your significance,
your powerful, inspiring presence.
I am awed as the gods welcome
the coursing of the natural flow
of your fresh life across the land.
I want to hold you forever and
yet, there is no sense to even try—
perhaps, your imprint is my gift.

At times,

I have imagined holding on
to loved ones, places, things—
even chapters of my life that
enlivened the sleeping giant
in the deep bed of my soul.
I know sweet gifts of living,
like sharing this life with you,
will never leave heart's banks.
Therefore, I will tenderly hold
dear treasures each gift defines.

Meanwhile,

As I gaze into sparkling pools
of your curious, cosmic eyes,
maybe the treasure I see in you
is that which I can give myself—
trust no matter my seasoned age,
I lay my life open like a river
whose nature deems no shelter,
nor ways to withhold its path,
or to keep ripples of light from
reflecting radiance in the world.

Therefore, remember my child,

The gods do not deem ways to
withhold your divine creations,
now dare I ask, *Not even mine?*
Thus, might our lives emulate
grand rivers, flowing freely,
converging watermarks with ease.
Might we create unique, rare
tributaries in this world because
our souls joined in the journey,
flowing to the ocean of eternity.

Body Temple

Reflecting on my mother's 92 years,
I bow reverently to the essence
of the woman of my beginning—
who willingly nurtured Divine seeds
to create my way.
I prayerfully breathe in gratitude
for the gift of her body temple
that offered my life.

Beholding her sacred fullness—with child,
she knew when her all had been given.
When the miracle that was meant to be
could no longer be withheld,
she birthed my life with might and courage,
releasing in cries of completion,
letting go from the well
of her warm water and nurturing blood.

Now, after decades of living,
I prayerfully breathe in gratitude
for the gift of my body temple
that continues to offer me life.
As a seasoned woman
impregnated by years of living,
I behold my own sacred fullness—with sage,
anticipating birth of another great purpose.

From creations cast by the sacred thread
that flows from the One Great Fertile Womb,
from generations of the past
into the greater good of the future . . .
comes urgency to birth Wisdom's legacy
for the eager evolution of this soul
that whispers its desires
in the heart of my body temple.

Consecration

In her most frail, dire days,
she prayed for me, her child,
blessed her grandchildren,
consecrated great-grandchildren,
born and yet to be born.
With her graciousness,
she welcomed fleeting moments
to affirm her love.

While the sweet ones hovered,
she blessed me,
sanctified me,
as she wiped my tears.
What more could I ask for
than her consecration—
that her god glorify my life
and all that I do, forevermore?

What more could I ask for
on this earth
than to be blessed by my Mother?
What more could I ask for
than to witness
her plea to the Sacred
to cradle my life eternally
while she journeyed on?

Dawning

I walked Bear Creek trail
as beams of first light
birthed another blessed day,
as its gentle glow released
quiet darkness of night.
Subtle images of many ears
and legs of nature's elders
gracefully stirred,
curiously watched,
welcoming me
to their wooded sanctuary.

I heard crisp, clear calls
yet, did not see their source,
walked along wet footprints
not knowing where they led,
tasted the morning's mist
unclear of what was beyond,
breathed in fresh whirring air
from eager, ascending wings
as I pondered my own instinct—
a sense
that I, too, was rousing.

A soft sigh escaped my lips
as rustling of nature's elders

Continue

115

awakened ancient wisdom in me,
stirred my own elder dawning,
rising after many days,
nights, and years
traversing this intricate life.
Then, I saw through dawn's mist
an image of my soul
on her knees, giving birth
to another dawning light.

For the Children

May you always have passion for life
and revere all living things.
May you always be inspired
to bring your unique creative energies into form.
May you always honor your power of choice
and respect the greatness
that resides within you.

May you always be tempted to courageously glimpse
into new depths of your soul,
embrace the magnificence of your bright light,
and not be afraid of your own dark corners,
remembering wisdom of the half moon
teaches the necessity of dark and light,
which is inherent to wholeness.

May you tenderly care for your body,
trust your mind, listen intently to your spirit.
May you understand that you
are the author of your wisdom, your joy and love.
May you live with a peaceful heart
and a healthy discontent to continuously seek,
ever-transcending into your best version of you.

I pray that you intuit that the world needs you,
your contributions,

Continue

117

your choices,
and your legacy.
I pray that you are confident
that your life matters
and shines forth with inspired purpose.

I pray that whatever or whomever your god is,
or becomes,
there is an unshakable knowing deep in your soul
of a loving Divine Presence in the universe—
or multiverses, for all we know,
that also resides eternally at the core of your being,
caring deeply about you and the flow of your life.

Last, and not least, remember . . .
I will always be with you
as you progressively learn to live in freedom
as your *true Self.*
You will never be alone.
I will always be in tandem, by your side,
in this world and in the next.

Grandchild's Stardust

Shimmering luminosity burst
into scattered fiery fragments.
Mystery gathered stardust
sending forth your ray as
the Sacred transformed light
into a sea of water and love,
breathing essence into you
for your birth into this life.

You came, I caressed you,
gazing with star-struck eyes.
I laid you on my awed heart
and a sea of love for all days
swept into my ardent soul.
There, you gifted an anchor
for my life-long purpose
as your seaworthy sage.

You are air for my breath,
words that I cannot speak,
lyrics for unwritten songs,
joy I cannot even quantify.
You fill me with conviction,
with flourishing hope for
the evolution of brilliance
only supernovas now bear.

Continue

As far as stardust goes—
have I seen luminous stars?
Yes, yet not beheld anything
like radiant beauty that you,
dear grandchild, shine forth
from your own sea of love—
illuminating hope and grace
for a grateful, eager world.

In Our Sacred Time

My brother died young
at thirty-five.

He used to ask me,
again and again,
for another glass of water.
I pretended to not want to—
yet, I adored him and
simply fetched more water.

As kids, at mealtimes
we lingered after others
left the worn kitchen table.
Our child eyes danced
in the space between us
and we would simply laugh.

It was our sacred time—
glasses full of water,
hands banging the table,
air echoing our laughter,
fire in our child hearts,
joy from our kindred souls.

I used to ask my brother,
again and again,
for advice about life.

Continue

121

I trusted him—yet knew
somehow wisdom came
from my own deep well.

Now, staring through
the windowpane beyond
the old kitchen table
in the abandoned room
in my mind, once again
memories usher grief.

My tender heart quickens . . .
How might I bring
life-giving gifts to others
in this dear, sacred time?
I listen—seeing in my mind
his kind, benevolent heart.

Love and respect others—
bring water for their glasses,
strong metal for their tables,
sustain pure air for laughter,
tend fire for their passion,
share joy for hurting hearts.

His sweetness welled inside
as I breathed my prayer,

Lead me to those who need
life-sustaining gifts
like water, . . . like joy
like we had in our sacred time.

And, my brother
simply whispered, *Yes,*
as I felt him next to me
sitting in the empty chair,
gazing out the window
in my mind.

Journey of Death

I want to know…
why are you afraid
of death?
Why do you shrink
from its word?
Where is the wisdom
in denying our birthright
to its sacred passage—
a path that must be
as miraculous
as coming here
in the first place?

What do you think
when you see
in your mind's eye
your father's sperm
and mother's ovum
diligently traveling
to create you?
Or more so,
even the spark—
or the thought
of you,
before your beginning?

What do you think
imagining the journey

you forgot—
from conception to body
growing exponentially
moment by moment
in a dark, warm,
watery womb
where your life
depended on a woman
sharing her heat, blood,
food, water and oxygen?

What do you think
picturing the courage
you mustered,
urged by circumstances
greater than you,
moving through darkness
smaller than you,
pushing into the light,
seizing that first breath
as air filled your lungs,
in this totally
foreign place?

What do you think
when you hear
in your mind's ear
your very first cry…
a cosmic cry,
announcing your arrival

Continue

125

in a life
you could not
have envisioned—
adventures and relationships,
experiences
awaiting your discoveries?

What do you think
when you reflect
on all the ideas,
hopes and dreams,
even quests
that you,
only you,
have manifested
in this world—
all a vacuum
without form
before you were born?

What do you think
when you pause
and reflect
with gratitude
the love and joy,
happiness,
the pain and sorrow,
disappointment
that grant a full
rainbow spectrum

of what it is to be alive
here on earth?

What about this dimension—
an outrageous,
inconceivable place
compared to
your once
simple stardust?
Can you dare believe
death's journey
may invite you again
into absolute magnificence
as Divine light streams
toward you again?

Could it be death is
our supreme experience
of true love
from which
we again dream
an unbelievable dream
of a life
we do not know?
Tell me what you think
while I sit here,
drinking my tea,
wondering.

Moments in the Dance of Life

That afternoon, bundled against the wind,
we watched glistening waves roll in
on the beach and recede back into itself.
Close by, others gathered in a circle
with bare feet, boots, sandals, high heels,
four leashed dogs in knit sweaters, and
a young man holding a red metal box.

Near them, our quick hands dug sand,
one scoop at a time, each one deeper
into the damp beach of ancient grains,
imagining a magical castle to appear.
Wind whipped my jacket as I turned,
noticing a dead young seal, beached,
interrupting me with a pinch of grief.

Came "Elliott" swaggering, sniffing along
while his master warned little children
of his deafness, blindness, and uncertainty.
"Jackie" followed like a bouncy fur-ball,
tumbling into our castle hole, eyes bobbing,
tongue flapping, with exuberant joy as
her old woman, cane in hand, smiled on.

Those gathered edged across the sand
like a tenuous human wave anticipating

yet more loss in search of elusive closure.
One by one, they reached in the red box
appearing to pray into the gray ash before
sprinkling remains of blessed life on water,
then circling their hands, washing grief.

Along side them, we gathered rocks—
gray, speckled, black, green, eclipsed,
tossing them one by one into plunks,
watching each stone's robust splash.
Among stones, a perfect seal skull lay
inviting more moments of reverence
for a life once living this rare reality.

I wrote my little granddaughter's name
in the sand with a play rake, then added
a preceding "I" and heart before her name.
Giggling, she aspired to her own message,
just as three blue heron flew above us,
swaying broad feathered spans in union,
landing in perfect breathtaking harmony.

In tenuous moments, the young man
turned the red metal box upside down
and scattered last granules of someone.
Then, a red ball cap and red handkerchief

Continue

129

were tossed into the oblong, whitish hue
floating atop the rising tide . . . pausing . . .
ready to set sail with gods of sea and light.

Dogs barked, the heron statues fished,
cool mist fell, gulls picked the seal pup,
the castle caved in, the perfect skull tossed,
the tide pitched rocks back onto the beach,
my granddaughter called out my name,
people walked hunkered in the cool wind,
hand in hand, each holding each tenderly.

We savored time, sitting quietly, silently
in a roughly-crafted log beach fort.
Abundant fragrance filled my nostrils
from the sweet plethora of wild roses
magnificently full bloom in the dunes.
The question came: *How do we dance
more intimately with this beloved life?*

In those woven moments, I whispered,
How do I dance?
How do I walk?
How do I play?
How do I pray?
*How do I give more intimately to this
exquisite lover called life?*

How do I offer myself for greater good,
love others well,
live generously in this precious world
until . . . they cast my red silk scarf
to the gods of wind and light
and circle their dusty hands
in the sea's glistening, ebbing tide?

My Child

You, my daughter,
carry in your mind
my spirit of seeking,
in your bones
my spirit of wisdom,
in your heart
my spirit of love.

You
came to me, called
by passion of my soul
longing for more,
further than myself,
in gifting the world
beyond my life.

You
carry me past
my future into yours,
expanding afar
my grandest imagination
with your own
exquisite spirit.

You
take me with you
into many tomorrows,
transcending into
that ever-continuing
sacred thread of
Wisdom's legacy.

No Thing Left Undone

I shall not fall on my knees
praying to the gods
for forgiveness—
for all I have not lived,
for all I have left undone.

Nor will I beg that this one life
truly mattered—
regardless of blindly chosen paths
or naive voices in my head.
Nor will I offer prayers for things
left incomplete in my hands,
incomplete in my heart.

Rather, I will pray to the gods
to give me one more chance
to serve others passionately,
to clear any misgivings,
to create a legacy of good,
and perhaps die while kissing
their precious, blessed earth.

I shall live each day believing
I will use up my life well,
leaving no thing left undone,
for me, for you . . .
for this generation or the next.

Orb Weaver's Tale

The morning air was still.
Barely a leaf moved as she lifted
her chocolate head toward sunlight.
She was a beauty to behold
as her long, brown hairy legs
pranced around a spiral wheel.

Tiptoeing seductively,
stopping here and then
in the intricate web,
she seemed to admire her masterpiece.
Perching on the crisscross band,
she knew her lover would come.

Yes, he would—and indeed
he gallantly appeared
with a gift at the edge
of the gate of sticky silk.
His gentle vibration tantalized her
as she slowly turned toward him.

He knew he would soon die
yet chose to enter the kingdom,
dancing into the dance of her life.
His need to amorously conquer
was too compelling to withhold
the ancient purpose of his palp.

Continue

There was no chance of survival.
Yet, they flirtatiously yielded,
winking back and forth, until—
in an instinctual moment—he fired!
Her claws, quicker than lightening,
grasped him in a spiral capture.

He stumbled, intoxicated with life,
surrendering to his offering of sacrifice.
She pounced him without hesitating—
and though in a tussle with time,
ceremoniously wrapped him in silk
as if life itself depended on *his* life.

The web shook as if to collapse
into the shiny red-tipped photinia.
Trembling soon faded into stillness.
The Queen of the Web quietly slogged
to the center of a world of solitude—
her oval belly full and pregnant.

Possibly, in those moments,
she even grieved that the dance
with her sweet lover was over—
although, it was a good day to die.
The forfeit made perfect sense, and
hers was yet to be, come Winter.

The tale of the orb weaver teaches
sometimes a life, or aspects of life,
need to die
so others can then live—
a worthwhile price for the sake
of orb children in a spiderling sac.

I want to know if you can be open
to radical natural consequences
inherent in the compelling dance
of your god-filled meaningful life?
Can you live purposefully, trusting
cycles of life, death and rebirth?

Can you honor the passing of parts
of your life that served you well?
Can you let go of old patterns
that stand in your way, reverently
wrap them with a bow of golden silk
and let them die—to feed your future?

Can you graciously surrender
to endings, and even to death itself,
knowing each has helped shape you,
what you are, who you are becoming?
Perhaps, the orb's tale reveals a holy task
in discovering the art of sage-mastery.

Pussy Willow Parable

In early dawn hours,
when fog began to loosen its hover,
the coolness of morning
evaporated puffs of my breath.

The mist released its tender embrace
around wintered pussy willows,
revealing emergence from solitude
in their weathered sleep.

Wet, white, plush crowns of two,
bound by their common red-hued pillar,
softened as the frosty condensation
relinquished its cradle.

Tiny sips clustered as a triumphant tear
birthed like a marvelous,
expanding mirror
clearly reflecting an upside down world.

Is it like it seems,
or is it not—

When we dare let go of what holds us
from birthing our marvelous,
expanding reflection
in what we perceive as an upside down world?

So, is it like it seems,
or is it not—

As a Sacred intelligence reflects
what is mystical, and welcomes
that which is incredulous, yet possible,
even after our own decades of winters.

Seeking the Sage

You seek beyond yourself
with a searching heart,
yet with a sleepy mind.
And, the wise sage asks,
For whom are you seeking?

You wander the fields
searching furrows and hills;
outward you go, ignorant
to the illusion of your desires,
Awaken from your sleep.

Befriend the quiet inside,
let your eyes grow large,
see the illuminating glow,
turn an ear to the soft voice,
Return to your own gate.

Nothing can compare to
the genius deep within—
wisdom gained from decades,
messages waiting to be heard,
It is the seeker who is sought.

Come to fully understand
that the one sought lives in
your own sacred homeland,
the one you are looking for,
The sage sought is you.

Standing in the Fire

Standing in the fire,
I pray it not go out.
My heart says,
Let it burn.
Let it engulf my thoughts,
my ideas,
and dreams,
each inspiration
that the muse has sparked.
Transform each into
unique beauty and art
of new stories
that desire to finally be born
out of the fires of creativity.

It says,
Stand in my fire.
Have faith in the flames,
blow breath on the embers,
don't let the author of your life
perish in cold cinders
because you were afraid,
or did not listen
with an open heart.

Trust the absolute genius
of that which longs
to be conceived by you,
that longs to be born
out of the fires of heaven.

Pray
Let it burn!

The Porch Swing

How do I want to leave?
Well, this is the way I'd prefer it to be—

It's a brisk autumn morning
late in October . . .
always my favorite month.
The trees are rich with color,
various shades of green,
mostly gold, crimson and brown.

The roses in the garden
aren't quite as gorgeous as in summer,
however, none of us are . . .
well, at least as far as delicacy goes.

Yes, there I am,
curled up on the old porch swing,
cozy still after all these years . . .
yes, now 40 some I suppose,
wearing that same favorite
old, tattered green sweater—

Wrapped up and loosely tied
around a now slight waist . . .
showing my behind smaller now
than when the sweater was new.

Nope, still no shoes on a brisk morning,
as I gaze at my toes
with slightly scuffed peach polish
from the pedicure
my precious daughter gave me
for my 97th birthday early this month.

Oh, a card from my sweet son's granddaughter.
She's fallen in love with life once again,
so much to offer the world . . .
that incredible great-grandchild of mine.

It's that luscious, red tapestry throw
draped across my lap
with beautiful stains from the past.
My coffee mug is smeared again
with a little light rosy lipstick
carefully placed earlier this morning.

A gentle moan and slow sigh
simultaneously escape my lips.
Shouldn't take Qi Gong so seriously,
I remind myself once again.

The swing moves a little as I catch the
weathered wood porch planks with my foot.
My coffee cup tips, spilling sweet aroma,
spotting my old, dog-eared book,

Continue

Radical Aging in a Wisdom Culture,
open to page 322 on the floral swing pillow.

The sun breaks through the fir trees
warming my wrinkled hands,
as I gaze at the aged veins
covered with fragile parchment skin.

Damn, I feel a little lightheaded again,
yet, it passes like a gentle smile.
My heart is content.
What more could I want
than to have loved well—
unless it was more of the same?

I hear the waves gently rush and recede
over the pebbles on the beach.
I see the birds twittering although
don't hear much they say anymore.

The salty morning air embraces my face,
caresses my thin white locks,
and the swing quiets . . . slowly quiets.
My little dog licks my face.
Could it be my brother waving to me?
Ah, it's been long since I saw their smiles.

Faintly, I hear the screen door open,
then gently close,
barely feel my beloved's tender kiss
moist on my now drying lips.

His hand smooths my un-furrowed brow.
And, the old swing quiets . . . quiets.
Then,
still as the morning fog . . .
tranquil,
a lovely silence comes.

I hear the gods whispering,
You have loved well.

The Sage Comes

After years and years,
finally . . .
the wise sage comes.

With compassionate acceptance
your sage welcomes everything back—
all you wished would be different,
old wounds, scars, and limps,
lost innocence, possessions, loves,
wildness you and others tried to tame,
dreams that remained formless,
fears that attempted conquest,
humiliation that nearly crippled,
grief leaving remnants of quiet anger,
confusion that disturbed your path,
relationships that eroded with time.

Time is what the inner sage says
is needed to finally understand
that all mattered, all was necessary,
for a deep, artful texture and
rich, transfixing, colorful grain
of your true divine magnificence
to emerge from the one and only
truly jaded shadow—
that is the horrific misperception

that you should have been perfect,
or whatever should be different.
No, not even so.

After years and years,
finally . . .
you will hear your sage speak.

Everything brought you to now.
Now, hold each morsel of your life
with tenderness,
honor as gems—
otherwise, wisdom is shamed,
unique creations are dishonored,
authenticity risks being aborted.
And, with tender self-compassion,
open to the great embrace
that allows immersion
into true love—you loving you,
that the gods gifted as only yours.

The sage says, this we do lest
we succumb to the madness
of severing ourselves from peace.
Thus, we must thank the wounds,
the scars, and the limps.

Continue

Choose forgiveness and love,
set free wildness that seeks
to ride dreams into new realities,
live passionately, confidently,
bid farewell to all that trusts not
the absolute beauty of our lives.
Then, graciously bow to wisdom—

That bequeaths the sage's call.

Vision of Sagessence

I come to you
to reveal a vision that
tumbles inside, condensed,
contained, living rib to rib.
Where shall be a next step?
Is it earth in our tread?
Or, an imprint yet to recede
into fresh, new, fertile soil?

Shall we rest in the settled dust
of culture's past knowing?
Or, lift our feet up
anticipating a daring turn?
Shall we tiptoe to the edge
of society's comfort and gaze,
or collapse into arms
of Wisdom's sacred abyss?

Turning our ears to muffled,
distant heart sounds, implore,
"Please retell the story that
the Ancient Ones prophesied."
Then comes a deep whisper
rising through dense history,
You are a sage; and
I bid your holy consecration.

Continue

O fervent sages—
draw from your wells,
illuminate your Sagessence,
shine forth your sacred story.
Enliven the cosmic story!
The breath of god awaits
to bless what only you can live . . .
yes, wisdom only you can give.

Be it, too, your vivid vision,
with your sacred flame aglow . . .
walking on, hands high,
and freedom
breathing in your soul,
assured
the breath of god awaits . . .
your Sagessence story.

REFLECTION

Fire in the Well

❀

As I reflect over the decades of my life, many wonderful experiences and many complex challenges inspired the compilation of my poetry. Poetry is prayer, poetry is passion, and poetry is a spiritual practice that provides openings for healing, discernment, enlightenment, and celebration. It can become a sacred path regardless of the belief, denomination, master, prophet, creed or spiritual expression to which one ascribes.

Poetry is a way of giving the soul voice. It speaks to many hearts other than the one that birthed it, and provides levels of inspiration at various times in the life journey. Whether the poet is seasoned in the art or not, inimitable words and unique meanings reflected in all poetry can only be delivered through each poet's authentic life and by their soul's voice. Therefore, I believe all poetry is extraordinary and unequaled in creation.

As sages deepening in authenticity, passion, compassion and vision, may we continue to gain fulfilling appreciation for the sacredness of all our life experiences throughout our miraculous, mysterious journey on Earth.

Blessings on the path of sacred poetry,

Marilyn Loy Every
Poet of Life

ABOUT THE AUTHOR

Fire in the Well

❁

Dr. Marilyn Loy Every holds a Doctor of Ministry in Wisdom Studies, with a focus on aging, and Certification in Spiritual Direction from Ubiquity University, San Francisco, California. She also holds a Master of Arts in Counseling Psychology from St. Martin's College in Olympia, Washington, a Master of Science in Audiology from the University of Wyoming, and a Bachelor of Science from the University of Nebraska. She specializes in aging issues, communication strategies, life transitions, loss and grief, and spiritual companioning with individuals and in sacred circle groups.

Marilyn Loy Every is visionary and founder of **Sagessence, LLC,** a company with a mission to develop and facilitate programs that inspire and prepare women and men to re-envision aging in the second half of their lives. She is passionate about promoting affirmative transformation of personal and cultural views that honor aging in our society so we may complete our lives with a most magnificent sense of meaningful fulfillment. Her belief is that in learning new possibilities in aging, embracing liberating images, and honoring change, we can more fully contribute to our communities and to the welfare of future generations.

Visit the Sagessence website at www.sagessence.com.

www.ingramcontent.com/pod-product-compliance
Lightning Source LLC
Chambersburg PA
CBHW022009090426
42741CB00007B/949